TOM EDISON FINDS OUT

A REALLY TRULY STORY BY
SADYEBETH AND ANSON LOWITZ
WITH ILLUSTRATIONS BY THE LATTER

68-2052

LERNER PUBLICATIONS COMPANY / MINNEAPOLIS, MINNESOTA

The Really Truly Stories

Barefoot Abe

The Cruise of Mr. Christopher Columbus

General George the Great

Mr. Key's Song

The Magic Fountain

The Pilgrims' Party

Tom Edison Finds Out

Second Printing 1968

Revised edition copyright © 1967 by Sadyebeth and Anson Lowitz

Original copyright 1940 by Sadyebeth and Anson Lowitz

Library of Congress Catalog Card Number: 67-29826

Manufactured in the United States of America

TO ALEXANDRA
of Michigan
and
TO THOSE
FOR WHOM
SHE WAS NAMED

PUBLISHER'S NOTE: Over a generation ago the Really Truly Stories were widely acclaimed by critics throughout the country and hailed as classics in the field of children's literature. Many parents and librarians have remembered these wonderful books and asked to have them published again . . . and that is what has happened. We take great pride in presenting this LERNER EDITION OF A UNIQUE CLASSIC for the enjoyment of a new generation.

Here is a real story about a real boy who started in, very young, to find
out just how things worked. His name was Thomas Alva Edison.
Mrs. Nancy Edison was his mother. Folks called his father Sam.
Sister Tannie was their oldest child. Next came big brother Will.
Tom was, by far, the youngest. His life began on February 11, 1847—
right in the midst of a blizzard!

The Edisons lived in a red brick house, in the town of Milan, Ohio.
They always had the best there was in furniture and such. Yet they had
    no electric light, no telephone, no phonograph—not even a radio!
    And they never went to the movies.

These things had not been thought up yet. So no one missed them much.

Tom was a skinny little boy. Everybody said they were sure that he was
    queer, with that enormous head. But when he grew up, he needed it,
    to hold all the things he knew.

Most every day he liked to play along the old canal. Once he got too close.
        In he fell! He learned about swimming from this.
The boatmen taught him all their songs. He remembered every stanza.

Tom kept mighty busy, from early dawn till dark, asking great big
    questions about all sorts of things. His father couldn't answer
    some. He did his very best. Then Tom would head for town.
He asked questions at the shipyards. He asked them at the mill.
    When he came in at suppertime, he was asking questions still.
Sam Edison just shook his head. It was most discouraging.

Tom was always thinking up something new to do. Once he saw a mother
  goose sitting on her nest. He gathered up a dozen eggs, sat down and
  tried it, too.
Another day he went exploring in a storehouse full of wheat.
In he tumbled! He huffed. He puffed. He coughed his way out.

In wintertime the old canal froze over smooth as glass. The first cold day
  the boys in town got out their skates to try them.
A friend whose skate-strap needed shortening asked Tom if he would help.
  Tom was glad to lend a hand.
The ax went up! The ax came down!! Tom's finger got the shortening!!!

Tom often wondered where things went when they were all burned up.
He thought a lot about it. The family barn looked pretty big. It
might help him find out. One match sent it up in a cloud of smoke.
Sam Edison didn't understand. He didn't even try. He led Tom down
to the village square. There he spanked him soundly.

Another thing that puzzled Tom was how the bees made honey. They just seemed to buzz around and sting and sniff at flowers.

Finding a bees' nest in a hollow fence post, Tom took a look inside. Out came the bees. They were very angry. They stung a ram who stood nearby. The ram chased Tom. Tom jumped the fence in a hurry.

In those days railroads were new. Folks in Milan didn't want one. They said the smoke would dirty things.   The noise would scare the horses. The railroad went to another town. So did Milan's business.

Sam thought the time had come to move.   He wanted to go to Michigan where he had been before. Port Huron sounded good to him. They'd try living there.   The Edisons steamed up to town on the *Ruby*.

Tom was only 7 when the Edisons arrived. They moved right into a nice
white house that stood on the old fort grounds.
Out back was the River St. Clair. Great pines grew all around.

Tom looked the place all over and decided it would do. With hide-outs
galore and fish at the door, he knew he'd have plenty of fun.

Sam Edison earned his living selling lumber, grain, and feed. But he liked to pick up extra cash from something on the side.

He built a tower on his land 100 feet in height. One could see from there to Canada, Lake Huron and the river. It surely was a sight.
Those who came to climb had to pay—25 cents a look. Few went up.
Tom perched there by the hour.

Somehow Tom never cared for school. The school cared less for him.
When his teacher asked him questions, he asked harder ones right back.
It was most upsetting. She'd never heard about such things. She said that
        Tom was crazy. After 3 months he left school for good.
Now, Mrs. Edison knew how to teach. She began again with Tom.
In no time at all, he'd read big books few grownups understood.

Mr. Edison paid Tom by the book for everything he read. The money went as fast as it came for chemicals and stuff. By the time Tom was 10, he had 200 bottles full in his basement laboratory. Each was labeled "POISON." Tom liked to mix and stir things up to see just what would happen. Some smoked. Some smelled. Often they exploded. His mother didn't like a dirty cellar. She made him keep it clean.

An older boy, named Michael Oates, worked for the Edisons. Tom often
tried things out on him. Once it was a powder that bubbled and made
gas. Tom was sure a dose of it would make a person fly.
Instead of going up at all, poor Oates thought he would die.

It took a lot of money to buy new things to try.   Now that Tom was 12, he thought it high time he went to work.   He wanted the job as newsboy on the train that ran to Detroit.   Mr. Edison said, "No!"
Tom begged and begged.   At last his father gave in.   Tom stocked up.

He sold papers, magazines, apples, gumdrops, tobacco, pipes, and nuts.

The trip to Detroit was 63 miles. It took 3 hours each way. Tom sold his
wares from coach to coach. Then he had nothing to do.
He tried reading magazines and papers from the first page to the last.
But that didn't use up his time. He could read a whole line at a glance.
So he moved his 200 bottles into the baggage car. There he set to work.

Tom earned good money on the train.   Often $10 a day.
He always divided whatever he made between his mother and his chemicals.
Each morning when he left for work he'd hand his mother a dollar.
His chemicals got the rest.

Tom knew everyone who worked along the railroad. The men who ran the telegraph he liked the best of all. They could answer questions.
In fact, he learned so much from them, he built a line from his house to a friend's. Electricity was all it needed. That was very scarce.

Tom tried making some by rubbing cats together.

Out of bed Tom bounced one day to send his morning greeting.
Alas! The line was out of order. He couldn't get one click.
Rushing to the window, he threw up the sash.
The family cow let out a "MOO." Tom's line was wound about her.

The train to Detroit spent most of the time at stations along the line. It never really got started before it was stopping again. One day Tom hopped off at Mt. Clemens to talk to Mr. Mackenzie. He ran the telegraph there. His little boy was playing on the tracks near by. Suddenly a loose freight car came rolling along—headed for the boy.

Tom dashed out and grabbed him, just in the nick of time.

Mr. Mackenzie was so very thankful he asked Tom what he wanted most. Tom said he'd like to telegraph as fast as Mr. Mackenzie. No sooner said than done. Each morning, Tom hopped off when the train pulled into Mt. Clemens. He hired a boy to sell in his place from there to Detroit and back again.

Mr. Mackenzie taught him all he knew. Soon Tom was teaching him.

Now, right at this time, our country was having a war with itself.   Brand-
new news was hard to get.   Each day crowds gathered at the railroad
station to hear what came over the telegraph.   This gave Tom an idea.
Buying some type and a printing press, he started the *Weekly Herald* in
the baggage car.   It was the first paper ever printed on a train.
At every stop Tom got fresh news.   His paper kept up to the minute.

Passengers all bought it. So did people at each stop. Tom sold 400 a week.
Oates met Tom every night and drove him home in the family wagon. Once,
as they passed the fort, Tom shouted, "Corporal of the Guard!"
A soldier came on the run. When he arrived no one was there. Next night,
it worked again. The third night Oates was caught. Tom ran for home!
The soldiers ran for Tom! He hid in a barrel of rotten potatoes.

Tom liked to make the most of his time. At every stop he'd hop off and sell until the train pulled out. One day, at Fraser, he was so busy, he nearly missed it. Rushing down the track, he tried to jump on.
A friendly brakeman grabbed him by the ears and pulled him all aboard.
From then on Tom was deaf.

The Port Huron train bumped along on a track that wiggled and twisted.
One day it wiggled too much. Off bounced the train. Papers, magazines,
    apples, gumdrops, tobacco, pipes, and nuts spilled in all directions.
Tom didn't believe in wasting things. He ate up all he could.
It took the family doctor to get him fixed again.

While in Detroit, Tom heard about a most important battle. Knowing folks along the line would want the news, he bought 1000 papers. Then he sent a wire to each town to say he'd be there soon with something extra special. Crowds at every station fought to buy his papers.

First he got a nickel. Next he asked a dime. Then he charged a quarter.

The Port Huron train kept on bumping along on a track that wiggled and
    twisted. Again it wiggled too much. Down came Tom's chemicals!
CRASH! BANG!! BOOM!!! Flames filled the baggage car.
The conductor was furious! First he put out the fire. At Smith's Creek,
    he put out Tom. It was a long way home.

Tom was very sad. Everything he owned was all mixed up on the station platform. Papers, bottles, magazines, type, apples, printing press, gumdrops, pipes, test tubes, tobacco, and nuts.

As soon as Tom could get a lift, he moved his belongings back home. There he started all over again.

The *Weekly Herald* grew and grew. Soon Tom took on a partner.
They changed the name to *Paul Pry* and printed stories about folks who
lived in town. A lot more people bought it.
Once Tom told things about a man that made the man real angry.

The man told Tom a thing or two and threw him in the river.

When Tom was 16 he got a job running the telegraph at Port Huron. He could send and receive with the greatest of ease. But messages were few. Then, right when it was needed most, ice broke the telegraph cable that ran under the river to Canada. A message simply had to be sent.

Tom thought and thought. Finally, he asked for a locomotive. With long and short toots he blew the message across.

Tom next worked nights, in Canada, for $25 a month. Every hour, all
    night long, he had to signal to his boss that he was still awake.
Since he spent his days inventing things, this left him short of sleep. So
    he made a machine out of his clock that sent his signal for him.
When his boss signaled back, Tom would never reply. It was most peculiar.
A man was sent to find out why. He found Tom fast asleep.

Tom was badly scolded and told to stay awake.
Alas! Alack! Another night he slept right through a message!
It nearly caused a wreck! The Toronto manager told Tom to come at once!
Tom knew that he would lose his job. He might even go to jail!
Finding the manager busy with friends, Tom thought it best not to wait.
So he slipped away and headed straight for home.

Since Port Huron didn't offer Tom the kind of work he wanted, he thought he'd see America. First he went to Indianapolis. Next he stopped off at Cincinnati. Then he wandered down to Memphis for a job.

Now, the men in Memphis liked to play jokes. They knew that Tom was new. So they asked him to take a message from the fastest man around. Tom took every word and wired back, "Try sending with your other foot."

For 5 whole years Tom tried out towns. At last he came to Boston. He didn't
own a cent. Five minutes after he arrived, he had a job.
This office served its drinking water in a nice big bucket. The dipper was
supposed to hang above it. Few remembered. So, just to remind them,
Tom wired the dipper. Anyone who took it down got an awful shock!

Each day when Tom came to work he brought his lunch along. The other men did, too. They always left their lunch boxes on a certain table.

The office was old and not very clean. It had a couple of roaches. When they learned how good these lunches were, they invited all their friends. Tom put wires around the table and shocked the roaches to death.

When Tom was 21 he invented a voting machine. Off he rushed to Washington.
Surely Congress could use it. It would save a lot of time.
Alas! Congressmen then were the same as they are now. They liked to take
their time. A voting machine was exactly what they didn't want.
After that Tom decided to invent only things everybody needed.

One summer Tom made gun cotton in a new and different way.
Not having time to try it out, he put it on a shelf behind the stove.
    Then he forgot all about it.
When the stove was lighted, it blew up with a BANG!

Most every cent that Tom could spare he'd spend on great big books.
Each night he'd read at least one book. Some nights he'd finish two.
Often he would just stay up and read the whole night through.
Then, without waiting to change his clothes, he'd run all the way to work.

Tom gave up his Boston job to spend all his time inventing.
Inventing was nice but it didn't quite pay. Soon he left for New York
to look for a job. When he got there his pockets were empty.
Three days later he was in the office of the Gold and Stock Telegraph
Company when their sending machine broke down. After their own
men had failed, Tom stepped up and fixed it. He was hired at once.

Tom's new job paid $300 a month. This was so much money he worked 20
    hours a day to make sure he really earned it. He did such good work,
    the head of the company asked Tom to improve the stock-telegraph.
Instead, Tom invented a brand-new kind. He hoped to get $5000 for it.
When he was handed a check for $40,000, he nearly fainted.
He went right to the bank to get his money and sat up all night to guard it.

With this money Tom started a factory all his own.   He was only 23.
At first he just made stock-telegraphs.   Then he thought up other things.
He also helped Christopher Sholes finish up inventing the typewriter.
The factory had day and night shifts.   Tom was foreman of them both.
He picked up sleep whenever he could, a half-hour at a time.

Six years later Tom moved his factory to Menlo Park, New Jersey. By this
    time he'd invented so many things most folks called him Mr. Edison.
Without waiting to get settled, he started inventing again. He fixed up
    Mr. Bell's telephone so it really worked much better and he added
    some improvements all his own.
Things he found out then are also used on radios today.

Among all the things Mr. Edison made, he liked the phonograph best. He thought of it while trying to build a telegraph that would take down messages on records. Perhaps he could put voices on records instead of dots and dashes. Quickly he drew a plan and had a model built.

To test it, Mr. Edison said, "Mary had a little lamb."

The phonograph talked right back, "Mary had a little lamb."

Next, Mr. Edison tried to make an electric light. Night and day, for 2
    whole years, he worked. He tried all sorts of ways.
At last, on October 21, 1879, he made a lamp that burned.

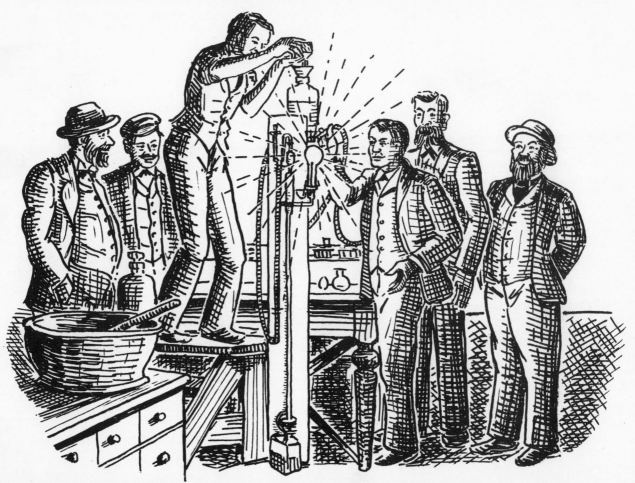

Tom Edison found out about a lot of things in all the years he lived.
Talking movies, dynamos, storage batteries and trolley cars were just a few.
But of them all, his greatest deed was when he gave us light.